*

Chaotic Harmony

By

J.J. BHATT

ISBN:

9798366926768

Title:

Chaotic Harmony

Author:

J.J. Bhatt

Published and Distributed by Amazon and Kindle worldwide.

This book is manufactured in the Unites States of America.

Recent Books by J.J. Bhatt

(Available from Amazon)

HUMAN ENDEAVOR: ***Essence & Mission/ A Call for Global Awakening, (*****2011)**

ROLLING SPIRITS: ***Being Becoming*** **/A Trilogy, (2012)**

ODYSSEY OF THE DAMNED: ***A Revolving Destiny,*** **(2013).**

PARISHRAM: ***Journey of the Human Spirits*****, (2014).**

TRIUMPH OF THE BOLD: ***A Poetic Reality*****, (2015).**

THEATER OF WISDOM, ***(2016).***

MAGNIFICENT QUEST: ***Life, Death & Eternity,*** **(2016).**

ESSENCE OF INDIA: ***A Comprehensive Perspective,*** **(2016).**

ESSENCE OF CHINA: ***Challenges & Possibilities*****, (2016).**

BEING & MORAL PERSUASION: ***A Bolt of Inspiration*****, (2017).**

REFELCTIONS, RECOLLECTIONS & EXPRESSIONS, (2018).

ONE, TWO, THREE... ETERNITY: ***A Poetic Odyssey, (*****2018).**

INDIA: ***Journey of Enlightenment*****, (2019a).**

SPINNING MIND, SPINNING TIME: ***C'est la vie*****, (2019b).Book 1.**

MEDITATION ON HOLY TRINITY, ***(2019c), Book 2.***

ENLIGHTENMENT: ***Fiat lux*****, (2019d), Book 3.**

BEING IN THE CONTEXTUAL ORBIT: ***Rhythm, Melody & Meaning, (*****2019e).**

QUINTESSENCE: ***Thought & Action,*** **(2019f).**

THE WILL TO ASCENT: ***Power of Boldness & Genius,*** **(2019g).**

RIDE ON A SPINNING WHEEL: ***Existence Introspected, (*****2020a).**

A FLASH OF LIGHT: *Splendors, Perplexities & Riddles,* (2020b).

ON A ZIG ZAG TRAIL: *The Flow of Life*, (2020c).

UNBOUNDED: *An Inner Sense of Destiny* (2020d).

REVERBERATIONS: The *Cosmic Pulse,* (2020e).

LIGHT & DARK: *Dialogue and Meaning,* (2021a).

ROLLING REALITY: *Being in flux, (2021b).*

FORMAL SPLENDOR: *The Inner Rigor,* (2021c).

TEMPORAL TO ETERNAL: *Unknown Expedition,* (2021d).

TRAILBLAZERS: *Spears of Courage*, (2021e).

TRIALS & ERRORS: *A Path to Human Understanding*, (2021f).

MEASURE OF HUMAN EXPERIENCE: *Brief Notes,* (2021g).

LIFE: *An Ellipsis (2022a).*

VALIDATION: *The Inner Realm of Essence* (2022b).

LET'S ROLL: *Brave Heart,* (2022c).

BEING BECOMING, (2022d).

INVINCIBLE, (2022e).

THE CODE: *DESTINY,* (2022f).

LIFE DIMYSTIFIED, (2022g).

ESSENTIAL HUMANITY, (2022h).

MORAL ADVENTURE, (2022i).

SPIRALING SPHERES (2022h).

EPHEMERAL SPLENDOR, (2023a).

CHAOTIC HARMONY, (2023b).

Preface

CHAOTIC HARMONY: That is essentially is the state of human being throughout history and continues even today and will do so in the future. The chaotic milieu is characterized by the constant conflicts, debates and the trial by existence while the realm of harmony defines the inner being where curiosity, creativity, compassion, hope, freewill and happiness keeps battling in favor of the whole to be illuminated.

Well the eternal struggle as mentioned between chaotic and harmonious nature of humans is poetically expressed in the book to inspire the young minds to identify, "Who they are and what they can become."

J.J. Bhatt

Contents

Preface 5
Adventure.............. 11
Spark 12
Existence............. 13
Renewal 14
Veritas 15
Genuine 16
Reflection............... 17
Confession 18
A Consequence........ 19
In the wing........... . 20
Will to Win........... 21
Time Travelers....... 22
Trust 23
Growth & change..... 24
Nostalgia 25
Amnesia 26
Riders 27
Matrix 28
Essence to be........ 29
Reckoning 30
That It Is.............. 31
Voyager............. 32
Epiphany 33
Keep going.......... 34
Dance with me.... .. 35
Eternal 36
Becoming........... 37
Turning Point....... 38
The Story........... 39
Identity 40
Sacred.............. 41
Lost.................. 42
Introspection.......... 43
Invitation 44
Rhythms..............45
Meaning 46
An abstraction...... 47
Being & Time....... 48
Gratitude............. 49
Foresight 50
Being & Truth...... 51
Self-knowing....... 52
Force within......... 53
Be Smart............. 54
Aliens................ 55
The Mission 56
Destiny 57
First Cause......... 58
First Dance 59
Thoughtless 60
Will Power 61
Endurance 62
Great wheel 63
Being As Is 64
First Step 65
Stay Focus 66
What If 67
In Love 68
Brave Child 69
Inner Voice 70
Illumination 71
Red Alert 72
Our Time 73
Conscience.......... 74
The Frame 75

Fortitude 76
The Journey 77
Deception 78
To Be 79
Consequential...... 80
The Gift 81
History Singing..... . 82
Noble Way 83
A Measure 84
Challenges......... . 85
Great Leap 86
Great Ride......... 87
The Path 88
Forever............ 89
Overture: 2022.... 90
Magic Seeds....... 91
On the Road...... 92
Open Book 93
Everlasting 94
Cauldron......... 95
Anticipation...... 96
Our Vows.......... 97
Will to Live....... . 98
New Direction 99
Moral Call...... .100
Humanity...... .101
Dignity......... .102
Immortal 103
We Dare......... 104
Contextual....... 105
You're.......... 106
Instinct........ . 107
Off the slumber 108
Off the mark. .. 109
Welcome........ 110
Gaia 111
Reality As Is....... 112
Life in motion..... 113
Cross-road 114
Young Braves..... .. 115
Our Story 116
Take Note 117
Conundrum......... 118
Freewill... 119
A Jolt 120
Soul Singing......... 121
Universal 122
Life Medley......... 123
High & Low 124
North Star........... 125
Silent Song 126
The Trail............. 127
Prayer 128
Inseparability 129
The Big Q 130
Eternal We're 131
Weird Way...... ... 132
On the Run......... 133
All in flux........... 134
Unstoppable........ 135
Juggernaut......... 136
What do I 137
Declaration......... 138
"I" Matters 139
Swimmers......... 140
Flashes 141
Old Habits......... 142
Aporia..............143
Green vs Greed.....144

Spin of a Wheel 145
Wounded Souls......... 146
Explorer................... 147
Determined Will......... 148
Song Forever 149
The Premise 150
Purity 151
"I" an Idea 152
Not yet.................. 153
Enigmatic 154
Background........... 155

Adventurer

It’s about
His nature,
It’s about
His destiny

Being,
What an eternal
Chaotic harmony
Still keeps rolling
Along the path:

To know
His own truth
Yes, it’s about
To unfold, “All
That Is”

It’s all
About clarity
And be bold
And creative for
His own good…

Spark

While
Ascending through
The mysterious
Reality

Does he ever
Realized, "He's
The wonder of all
Wonders!"

While
Flying from one
Unknown to another

Does he ever
Realized, "He's
The time traveler
Passing
Through his own
Thick and thin!"

While
Being immersed
Into the world of
"Silence"

Does he ever
Know, "He's the
Cosmic spark in the
Mighty Universe."

Being & Existence

If each is
A renewed spirit

Wouldn'that be
The first step
To their freedom

If each is
An overture:
Supreme creativity

Wouldn't
It lead to their
Waiting truth

If all spirits
Walk along the
Path called,
"Moral courage"

Wouldn't
That actualizes
Their common
Destiny...

Renewal

Behind
Suffering there is
Always that self
Awakening

If he
Exercises
His will to change
The course

To that
We say, "Epiphany,"
What is a sudden
Connectivity with the
Inner being itself

Yes,
That is where
His reason and
Understanding resides

And from,
There he begins the
Real journey at last...

Veritas

Life be
Balanced well
Between chaos
And order

Life be
Weighed well
Between what's
Right and what's not

After all
We're
Consequential
Beings with every
Thought, word and
Action impacting
Our will

Let life be
Glow of the
Mind to fulfill all
Possibilities to know

Let
The meaning
Of being
Be in laughter,
Love and joy with
Billion others too...

Genuine

Tranquil
Minds
Eternally in
Communion with
All-inspiring universe

They
Remain
Constant in the world
Of growth and change

Tranquil
Souls eternally
In communion with
The Moral Self

They remain
Steady
In their journey
To the
Ultimate Truth

That is the
Rhythm of their
Existence

That is the
Essence of their
Inner Being…

Reflection

Often
Thought the finite
And Infinite are equal
And eternal

Yes, at deep
Reality
That we ought to
Known

This Soul
So silenced forever
Still to be understood,
Silently well

What is the
Point to keep dancing
In the conceptual darkness
When light is everywhere
In the universe

I ask,
"What is the reason
Why we keep denying
Our well deserved destiny
To the realm of Becoming

And, why keep
Rotting into this world
Full of constraints and
False narratives and be
Nobody till we hit the
Dead end…

Confession

It's been
A long waiting in
The company of her
Dream

So I now say,
In this reality,
" Darling, I am in
Love with you"

It's been
Long to come to
This point to express
My feelings before
You, face to face

After a long
Struggle, now I stand
Before you fearlessly
And confess, " I am
In love with you and
I ask you to be mine…"

I know,
It's you alone to
Say, "Either yes or no"
And, I shall wait for your
Response, either now or
Never; I've just expressed
My soul to you.."

Consequential

Tomorrow
Keeps revolving
Constantly and
Why am I not
Moving?

Past keeps
Chasing the present
And why
Am I not thinking
Of consequences!

All is ephemeral,
All is illusive and all
Is going to die one day

Let I wake-up,
Let I turn the alarm,
At once and let I
Make the first move

It's a repeating
Drama; rolling
From known to the
Unknown and seems
No escape to the end…

Waiting

It’s been a
Long wait to
Confess my deep
Feelings,

So I say
Darling, “I am in
Love with you”

Many seasons
Gone by
While I’ve
Been gathering
My courage

To say,
“Darling
“Would you be
Mine!”

Will to Win

Sleep well
Tonight dear child
For the journey
Tomorrow shall
Be arduous and long

Play well
Today
While you can for
The big game shall be
Quite challenging,
Tomorrow indeed

That's the
Price to be paid by
Everyone being born
Human

Don't be in
Despair for you're
Blessed to be the
Fearless inner being

Keep walking
With your magnifique
Universe of integrity,
Positivity and a
Determined will and
Learn, "How
To win the game."

Time
Travelers

We
Made it all
The way didn't
We dear

We beat
All the odds and
Were triumphant in
In the end, didn't
We dear

Why then
Feel guilty and
Be in tears?

Life is
The realm of
Constant challenges
And
You can't be afraid
And run away from
The scene

Come,
Dear heart and
Let us roll ahead with
Full-confidence in the
Name of love and love
Alone as our strength…

Trust

Sweet Heart,
Don't say,
"The journeys
Over"

Don't say,
"It's end of
The world"

Let us
Be brave and
Regain dream and
The feelings

Yes dear,
We're being tested
At this critical time,
Let us keep our
Trust intact

Let us
Just keep the
Journey rolling with
Calm and alert…

Growth & Change

When
We're young,
Saw the world so
Beautiful and full
Of vigor

When
We're in love,
All seemed shining
With hope and joy

When
We're hungry for
Wealth and fame;
Our attitude changed

Oh yes,
That was
When we're lost
On the highway,
Going nowhere

No wonder,
In the end,
We became,
Nothing, but ever
Struggling worms…

Nostalgia

At this very
Moment,
I feel loves flowing
Toward your world

Wonder,
What you must
Be doing today?

Do you
Ever remember
The days of our
Young adventures

Do you
Still sing the
Song we sang
Every spring to be
Ever

Time
What a magic
Wand that slipped
Away so mercurially

And we never
Got a chance to say,
"Goodbye"

Amnesia

There is a
War on as the
World has gone
Mad

And no one
Knows,
"What would be
The consequences"

That seems
To be the state of
Big time, "Apathy"

Are guardians
In-charge aware,
"What are they
Up to?"

Do us
Know, "Where
The worlds
Heading?"

Does any
One care,
There is darkness
Cascading over our
Children's dream…

Riders

Hey there
Friends,
We shall endure well
Through the thick and
Fog of our time

Let's just
Learn to hang-in
Together with our
Courage and hope

If we
Stand together
One, we shall be
The winners in no
Time

Damn right,
Let's endure to
Attain our mission
On time

Yes, friends,
Let's wake up to
The reality of these
Tough times …

Grand
Matrix

It's this
Grand matrix of
All that is

Where
Our quest begins
And never ends

Indeed,
That is
Existence in
Such a spinning
Grand matrix

We're
Born to be rolling
From known to the
Unknown and
That's a big
Challenge to meet

Oh yes,
That eternal riddle
Called, "Grand Matrix"
Is one paradox yet
To be cracked…

Essence To Be

Life's
Obfuscating
At every
Turning point and

Intelligent being
Still unknown to
His possibilities to
Fulfill the mission,
On time

Wonder,
If there is any
Difference between
Human purpose and
His destiny or what?

Where do we
Draw the line
Between trials of
Human condition and
His ideal dream to be…

Reckoning

People,
Happily singing,
Dancing and
Celebrating
Today

Let them
Feel good
For that is
The only way to
Keep riding all the
Way to the end

People,
Happy for a
Change as they
Wake-up from
Their illusion

People,
Happy knowing
They're all
Equal and heading
Toward the same
Dream…

That It Is

Each, but a
Part of cosmic
Whole

The whole
What is an
Absolute and relative
Building reality,
At once

Each,
An evolving soul
Bouncing between
Life, death and rebirth

Each,
Wrapped-up
Temporal into
Permanence ever

Each
Seeking freedom
From impermanence
And be the Eternal
Consciousness,
Simply…

Voyager

To be
Is a logical
Necessity
To own his
Meaning

Being alone
Must voyage
Through the
Vicissitudes of
Life and time,
Even when
The shore never
Nears to the eyes

To be
Is a
Moral necessity
Surely, that's his
Responsibility;

How
To steer through
Rough waters of
The stormy Sea…

Epiphany

In this
Serene Moment
Of quiescent

Where "I"
Born with a
Purpose and

That is
My justification
To be human

That is
The beginning of
My adventure and joy

That is
The fire of my
Moral being caught
Into the vagaries of
The time

Let go,
Vanity and greed
And let "I" be in
Harmony with the
Self and the world…

Keep Going

Who cares?
Whatever is the
Meaning in
This turbulence

Who cares?
Whatever is the
Condition of
Existence

Just pick-up
Lost dreams and
Get on with the
Noble mission

Let's not
Talk. Let's not
Debate and
Be afraid

Let's just
Leap forward
With our open
Minds…

Dance
With Me

Lady,
I saw
You're lovely
Eyes and decided
To dance with you
Whole night

Yes,
Dear lady
Hold my hand and
Softly dance with
My whole life

Look at
The Moonlit and
Zillion stars;
Smiling for you
And I

Hey dear
Lady, won't you
Give me your hand
And dance with
Me whole night!

Eternal

Million miles
To go and another
Millions waiting in
The wing

That's been
Journey of
The human spirit
Since beginning

All revolving
Around curiosity
And struggle

All beauty
And truth enhancing
His essence quietly

Million dreams
To be fulfilled
And millions still
Waiting in the wing…

Becoming

Come off
These feelings of
Despair and
Get the mental
Gear strong

Begin
The task with
Courage and
Determined will

Let's
Defeat
False narratives and
Dogmatic claims

And begin
Walking along
A terra firma

And drop all
Doubts and debates;
Taking charge to
Think of freedom
Next…

Turning Point

Turning
Point at every
Way when being
Sees the world
Differently

That is
The highway of
To roll from present
To the future

Let him
Not forget,
Future of
Children as well

Let him
Not sunk into
The habit of hedonism
And techno-opium

Yes, let him
Remain calm and alert
And keep the march
Going toward his very
Meaning…

The Story

We
First met wild
Wolves and
Slowly turned them
Into loving pets

We became
Fond of big
Cats and dare
Tame them to be
Our exotic friends

We even
Went after bears,
Monkeys and
Many others and

We
Never forgot to
Love them all

We grew up
To be civilized beings,
But failed, "How to
Love our own kind!"

Identity

While
Rolling along the
Garden of roses and
Thorns,

We're
On an expedition
Itself indeed

As we're
Unfolding our
Possibilities,

We're
Also stumbling
Over
The zigzag trail

Against
Such odds,
We're still
The essence of
All the unknowns;
To be understood…

Sacred

Every
Soul
Is an ever
Expanding
Consciousness

It's trying to
Be the light
Of the
Zillion stars

Yes,
That's the
Discovery of their
Meaning of the
Self

That's why
Every human
Be respected
Well, and

That's the
Essence of every
Human whose
Born here…

Lost

Great minds
Over the time gave
Us wisdom,
"What is freedom,
Social covenant and
General Will and so on"

Even
Pioneers of each
Faith asked to be
Good and to destroy
Evil always

Great saints
And seers
Inspired us to
Know our truth

Alas, in time,
We forgot "Who we
Are and what is the
Authentic meaning of
Our own being…"

Introspection

These
Dust storms full
Of confusions and
Subjective inferences;
Blocking clarity of
My Truth

These infinite
Objects in the
Wild Universe
Keep renewing
Reality; challenging
To walk through it all
In one life

Is it not the
Time to
Get away from
The thick layers of
Illusion and

Regain
Real sense,
"Who am I and
What I ought to be..."

Invitation

Hey
Dear girl,
Come and dance
With me

Yes, to
Enjoy
Beauty and truth
Of our feelings

Hey girl,
Don't ignore
This chance for it
Happens only once
In a while

Hey
Sweet girl,
Don't run away from
Our waiting hearts

I say,
"Let's dance
While we've this
Only chance…"

Rhythms

Freewill,
What a magic,
What a driving
Force

Ascending
"I"
To the highest
Meaning

Curiosity,
What a miracle,
What a genuine
Gift to be

Lifting "I"
To the sanctum of
My inner being

Life,
What a
Beautiful feeling
What a rhythm of
The efflorescent bliss…

Being & Meaning

Forgiveness
When exercised
Without a gain

At that
Point human
Conquers the mind

When
Clarity is grasped,
World is lifted to the
Highest Humanity, ever

When
Soul is powered
By Moral intention
And rational insight

Truth
Can never escape
From within

Let it be
The rhythm, the melody
And the noble inspiration
Of every willing will…

Abstraction

"That"
Simply is
"Brahman"

What is an
Eternally
Enlightened
Being

"That" is the
Source from
Where real and unreal
Projected to the mind

"That" is
Not a conventional
Divine, but the
Eternal consciousness,
Itself

"That" is
Freedom from
Dogmatic claims

"That"
What a total
Spirit; flowing from
Beginning to Beginning…

Being &
Time

Time is
Slipping away
Mercurially and
We're still stuck with
Old grievances' and
Trivialities

We've
Forgotten the
Roots of our true
Reality and

Brought
Forth nothing but a
World of bigotry,
Violence and war

Why we're
Ever so silent and
Keep living in the
Milieu of despair and
Anxiety

What an irony
Of our fate as time
Is slipping away and
The light seems so
Far from our
Wishes and dreams…

Gratitude

Every human
So born is the
Logical necessity
To discover the
Ultimate truth

Every human
So grown here is
The intelligent will to
Build a better world,
Of course

Let it be
The rational grasp
Of the noble mission
We've been on

Let it be
The First Principle;
Having this gifted
Chance and

Be born
On this beautiful
Planet Blue for
Some good reason…

Foresight

Why be
Burden by
These riddles,
Contradictions and
Stubbornness?

Time
To drop off all
Unnecessary
Baggage's now:
Envy, vanity,
Greed and
Many more

And pick-up
The real
Track heading
To the
Right destination

Where
Future shall
Be smiling forever
In the name of
Our kids…

Being &
Truth

What a
Wonderful
Feelings
To be alive and
Be creative

How
Exciting it's
To be active with
Curiosity and
New ideas

Oh yes,
So happy to be
Born human for
There're zillion
Stars to be kissed

At the
Surface all seems
So abstruse and
Fragmented and
In turmoil

Just
Take a deep dive
Into deep reality and
There is harmony in
The awakened Soul…

Self-Knowing

Million "Roses"
Smiling
With full gusto
Of love, life
Laughter, alright

Why then
Keep walking along
The trail where tears
And despair put up
Their signs

Million "Dreams"
Keep dancing in
Every head, but
Why aren't turned
Into happiness and
Hope!

Why not
Open-up the world
Of beauty and truth
For children
And theirs to come

Why keep
Rotting into this
"Divisional milieu"
For too long!

Force Within

Let it be
A long
Meandering
Journey

And let it
Never show
Mercy in return

In such
A pressing
Experience

Let the
Determined will
Never quits the

Where
Human character
Charters faith to
Succeed

Let it be his
Moral courage
Inspiring to lift the
Mighty mountains
Every time…

Be
Smart

Why
Keep aimlessly
Rolling along a
Winding road

Why can't
We care to read
Guiding signs posted
In the big prints

Driving this
Precious life without
A map and a set purpose
Is always hazardous to
The dream itself

Why can't
We pause for a
While and begin to
Read the map well and
Decide the very goal of
The journey we've been
On

Knowing
Where we're going
Brings pleasure to the
Planned trip and children
Too gets well educated
Also…

Aliens

What if
We're
The lost souls in
This alien realm

Where we're
Not supposed to
Be?

What if
We're marooned
In this world!

Is there
Any meaning to
Be here or what?

Is there
Any reason
To be here and
Why?

What if
This existence
Is but a blurred
Essence
Going nowhere or
What!

The Mission

Being human
Means a constant
Stream of consciousness;
Filling up all blanks of
Enigmatic reality,
What we think it is

Being human
Means an incessant
Historic experiences
Written from one
Generation to another
With grief and joy

Time to avoid
Blunders and be
Liberated from
Clutches of the
Tribal mindsets

Being human
Means taking moral
Responsibility toward
Next generation and
Others succeeding them…

Destiny

Why not
Be a
Steady bridge
Between known
And unknown

Why
Keep titling in
Favor of negative
Attitude most of
The time

Why not
Be at every
Turning point
To keep nourishing
This troubled being

Let
Life keep dancing
With love and love
Only
Until, we arrive
At the Temple of
Our genuine destiny,
At last…

First Cause

For a change,
Let human be the
“First Cause” and

Let the
New journey
Begin with a spirit
Of inclusion and
Dignity of all

For a change,
Let human be the
Divine of his
Inner being, at last

Let the
Bold odyssey
Begin with a new
Zeal of pure moral
Reckoning for sure…

First
Dance

All I know,
"I am in love
With you dear
Heart"

All is glory
To me when I
See you every
Time

Now
That you've
Begin to notice
My soul

I know,
"We're to be
United soon"

Let's not
Pretend as if, you
Don't me so well
And walk away
Every time

Come dear
Heart and face the
Consequence of our
First dance...

Thoughtless

Life is
Full of adventures
And struggles as well

Life
What an
Inspiration with
Fascinations that
I can absorb

Life
Always a
Wonderful cosmic
Experience

To be
Rolling from zero
To infinity without
A thought

Oh yes,
Life
What a splendor
Having born
In human form,
Indeed.

Will
Power

When
Sun sinks
Beneath horizon
And darkness
Cascades the world

In such a
State of reality,
I must hang onto
To my inner strength

Let darkness
Blind all there is
To know, but
I don't care

For "Silence"
Of the night is
My real pal

I shall
Prevail, I shall
Prevail always,
No matter what ever
The consequences of
This stygian night…

Endurance

I a
Natural rhythm,
Melody and meaning
Keeps rolling from
One beginning to
Another, always
Endless

And that is
The truth of every
Other cosmic being,
As well

Seems we're
Accidentally,
Thrown into the
Big Riddle;
Wrapped by the
Everlasting
Struggles

It's only
Through purity
Of conquered mind,
"There is genuine
Beauty and Truth;
Welcoming us with
Open arms…

Great Wheel

Enigmatic
Human is the
Name of the
Game

Being is
Immersed in
The quest of
Truth forever

That is the
Reality keeps
Him alive since
Beginning

All the
Objects either
Born or dying
In the universe;
Seeking clarity,
Always

And nothing
More is achieved,
But the
" Great Wheel"
Keeps spinning ever…

Being
As Is

Let
Fearlessness
Thrust him
Forward

Let
“Freewill”
Fly him off the
Edge

Yes,
Let him reach
Out to the
Distant stars
In this mighty
Universe

To get
The answer to
All his unknowns,

Let him
Live life with a
Purpose and
Be enlightened
Through his own
Struggles…

First Step

In this
Moon lit night
I am lost with
You while holding
Onto my dream

It doesn't
Matter any more
For your love is
All that was, that is
And that shall be

Yes,
Sweet Heart,
It's beautiful
Starry heavens
Smiling over our
Possibilities always

So
I invite you,
"Come and
Dance with me
For that is the first
Step to be"

Yes,
Sweet Heart,
That is the first
Truth of our very
Essence to be…

Stay Focused

Never be
Afraid, instead
Seek solution to the
Troubling issue on
Hand

Never try
To be somebody,
When you got the
Power to rise on your
Own

Damn right,
Never go after
People who fail to
Sustain your dignity

And, never
Repeat the same
Mistake over and
Again when
Humiliated once

Let the
Inner being be
Awakened and let
It define the right
Direction to glow…

What If?

What if,
“I” just an
Temporal human
Form

Once
“I” is gone, what’s
The significance
Of the left over
Urn

What if,
“I” just an
Illusion that has
Turned into reality
For a brief…

In Love

Dear Love,
You're the state
Of my zeal, thrill
And a never ending
Dream

That's just
The beginning of
My confession

Yes, that's the
Invitation to come
To my world where
Happy feelings are
Waiting for you and I

Dear Love,
Don't be afraid
For my world is
Waiting for your
Response

Don't let
This moment
Pass
Don't let the
Dream goes dry…

,

Brave Child

Dear Child,
Keep walking to
Your destiny with all
Courage and inspiration
You've in your inner
Spirit, always

Your
World shall be
Different tomorrow
And get ready to make
It through with your
Well awakened mind

Dear child,
Keep the focus
While on the trail
For there're many
Unknown turning
Points

Dear child,
Let your
"Will to Win"
Attitude shall
Help you
Get ready and be
Bold to roll….

Inner Voice

Looking
At the big mirror
Of intentionality

I suddenly
Became aware,
"My journey is an
Ascension
From potentiality
To actuality"

On close-up,
I begin to
Understand,

"I am
The arrow in
Flight heading
To the absolute
Objectivity
Called, "Self-
Realization"

Yes, am
The thought, the
Word and the action
Called, "Without
A loss of Truth,
S*alva veritate*…"

Illumination

When
Human emerged
Out of the lot and
Turned creative

He began
To ask, "What
Is the goal and
How to attain it"

That is
The essence of
His reflective mind

Human,
What an art in
Motion of romantic
And ideals born
To be
Shining forever…

Red Alert

When
The storm remains
So stubborn with
Mass confusion and
Constant bickering

Let the
Rational being be
Calm but alert at the
Same time and
Seek clarity in return

When
War mongers are
Busy stretching the
Blood spills intentionally
For profit and power
That never ending
Blunder be
Corrected at once

Let the
World Court
Of opinion resist the
War mongers before its
Too late to save
Humanity and the Planet
Itself…

Our Time

In these
Modern times,
Why we've not
Gain the lasting
Peace so far

I mean,
Why we've
Not become wise
In the age of
Information

I mean,
Where
We're already
One connected
Humanity at all
Time

Why
Ignore the
Situation and
Why don't
We correct the
Recurring sin!

Conscience

Without
Integrity
Of the mind

There is
No
Moral courage

Without
Honoring
Dignity of every
Being

There is
No escape
From the sinful
Existence

That is
The Silent Truth
That must be kept
Active while
Being in the human
Form…

The
Frame

All thoughts,
Ideas and whims
Keeps spinning
In our
3-lb machine

It constantly
Scans the world
And gives power
To know and to
Understand

What a
Magnificent is
This Grand Machine
Where every question
Has its answer in it

Viva la.
The Grand magic
Machine; keeping
Humans hanging
In-between
Known and the
Unknown,
Perhaps forever!

Fortitude

Opportunities
Be seized
When hit
By a crisis

That's the
Best way to exit
From suffering,
Guilt and regret

Instead,
Let hope and
Calm be the
Governing state of
The mind

When facing
Dark days of life
And time

Be smart
And be aware of
Of the real Self and let
Head-winds swirl by
Your time…

The Journey

We're
The creative art
Of ethical judgment
As we keep facing
Growth and change

We're
The riders of
Enlightened dreams
And must enjoy the
Journey while on

That is
Our mission
That is the way
To walk through
This assigned life
And time

Let the
Hidden force
Illuminate the
Collective spirits;
All the way to
Our Truth...

Deception!

Even
In this
Twenty-first,
Social justice and
Moral norms haven't
Come to conclusion
Yet

Intelligent
Beings, "Where
You are hiding
Today"

Great
Guardians,
"Why are you
So inept today"

Is there a
Global cry by the
Billions demanding,
"Quality air,
Dignity and privacy!"

To Be

If we just
Grasp a simple
Wisdom:

"Truth,
It is our soul,
Our substance,
Our nature"

With such a
Foundation, the
Walk must begin
On time

I mean, once,
We know the
Magic, the journey
Becomes bit easier

Come,
Let's gather
A greater strength
And sacrifice
Bit of our selfish
Comforts for the
Good of the whole…

Consequential

Life
What a
Trail of fragile
Experience
Driven by the
Thick and thin
Consequences

To be
A happy
Walker,
Let “Silence”
Balance order
And chaos at
Every turn

I mean,
While being
Alone along
The winding
Path of
No return

That may
Well be the
Unwritten
Inscription
Beneath,
“His Essence”

The Gift

Each a
Beautiful child
Born to be the
Master of the
Universe

Each
Is a vibrating
Cosmic message
To be unfolded
Through time

Let us
Relearn to give
Them
A genuine love,
Laughter and joy

No point
In ignoring the
Magic gift for
Each child is
Our future and
A continuum of
Our core Essence…

History Singing

History sings,
"You don't
Own God and you
Can't claim that's
Your right"

Just
Recall your
Deeds filled
With imperialistic
Modes

No you
Can't be called,
"Civilized" for its
Just a façade before
The world

That is the
Deep impression
And that is the
Real experience

Those who
Suffered under your
Imposed immoral rule

Sorry, history
Can't be stopped
From singing the
Truth…

Noble
Way

Being
Alone is the
Self evident necessity
To be the enlightened
Spirit

That is
The only way
For humanity to
Arrive at its ultimate
Goal

That is
The only hope
To open the door
To the total truth

Being
Alone must reckon
Perfection within

Let his/her
Noble endeavor
Keeps
Evolving forever…

A Measure

In the final
Analysis, it's the
Selfless love wrapped
Around with selflessness
Itself

Kicks the
Journey in its
Highest gear and
The world seem
So meaningful with
New lenses

On the
Way, there are
Light and dark
Patches to go
Through

But let your
Awakened mind
Holds it,
"All is beautiful and
Equal in unity of the
Spirit"

That is
The highway
Leading to the
Realm called,
"Divine is the
Human, indeed"

Challenges

How do
We reduce all
Lies and
Turn ‘em into
Ordinary truth

And how do
We flip the
Complexity into
A genuine simple
Clarity for sure

These are
The challenges
To be resolved
Before heading
North

I ask
Again, “How
Do we
Turn this human
Into one helluva
Moral Being!

Great Leap

Let's take
A leap of
Reason

Let's be
Brave and
Keep glowing

'Till we can
Vanish all the
Wrongs thus
Straighten up
Our thick heads

What
We're after is
Depth of our
Courage and
Wisdom at-best

Yes,
What we're
Seeking, "How to
Overcome all
Obstacles and be
Happily free."

Great Ride

Don't let
Anyone threaten
Your big dream

Don't let
Life despair you
Any more

For you're
Born to be great
In all respects

Never be
Intimidated and
Never let anyone
Rob your goal

Yes, that's the
Fearlessness, you
Must carry with you
At all time

Don't let
Anyone governed
Your thoughts, but
You alone

You're
Young and good
So keep courage and
Be steady while on the
Great ride…

The Path

Let
Freedom ring
In every human
Wanting to see the
World in Peace

Let it
Be the song of
Every man, woman
And child wanting
To dream big

Let
The echoes of
"Freedom"
Ring forever

And let
Humanity stands
Above all forever

Let the
Awakened spirits
Begin their
Moral mission,
From this point on…

Forever

Darling,
This life is
Our only chance
To be in love,
I mean today and
Now

Come and
Give a sweet smile
And be mine

Darling,
We're two spirits
Willing to be One

Why then,
All these fuss to
Avoid the inevitable

Darling,
Time is slipping
Away so quick
And life to be lived
Well

Give me
Your hand and
Let's begin the
Journey as One…

Overture:
2022

Existence
At times seem
Simply
An integration of
All lose ends

Human too is
But a revolving
Whims of his own

No wonder,
Why all lost
Souls keep banging
One another with a'
Lace of envy, vanity
And greed

Being,
What an
Intellectual
Mysticism still
Falling short of
His noble mission

What if
Humans are victim
Of vagaries of life
And time burdened
By the glorious
Blunders and sins…

Magic Seeds

Why be
Perplexed and
What for?

We're
The cosmic
Seeds born
And die to be
Born again

Whatever
Form or shape
We keep returning,
We never forget
The mission either
Big or small

Beyond
The petite mind,
All is pure beauty and
Truth through eternity
That yet to be known…

On the Road

They say,
“Human
Is an arrow in
Flight from known
To the
Unknown, alright”

They
Even says,
“He’s the lost soul
In the Universe”

Well,
He’s’ been on
Blue speck for
Sometimes

Is it not
High time,
He arrives at
The necessary
Moral maturity

And
Resolve all
Outstanding
Issues of his
Troubled
Existence…

Open
Book

It's been
A challenge
To be alive and
To seek truth
Alone

Life itself
What a
Big perplexed
Experience
Wrapped by the
Subjective
Inferences

It's been
Always a magic
To live through
The path of
Good and evil

Yes,
That's been the
Greatest test of all;
Making our essence
To be the best forever…

Ever
Lasting

In this
Infinity of all that is,
"I" the single speck
Keeps revolving with
A meaning

This reality,
What I conceive
Is the apex; standing
Upon a base so broad
And quite abstruse

Yet, am
Determined to
Reach out to the
Peak and turn it
Into one simple
Unity of all, but

I must begin
With a dot called,
"Zero" and keep
Ascending toward
"Infinity" and be the
Winner at last…

Cauldron

Today,
NEWS keeps
Popping up
Continuously,
Often twisted by
The self-interest
And greed

Nemesis
Is dehumanized
And the real culprit,
Of course is shown
Being a good guy

That is
How this
Fascinating, “Age
Of Information”
Keeps controlling
Our thoughts

No wonder,
There is so much
Confusion and
Growing friction
In the world

And
No one is
Listening while
Humanity keeps
Bobbing into the
Cauldron of fake news…
News…

Anticipation

All seems
Temporary caught
Into the frame of
Forever

Being too
Though temporal,
Dreams to be
Eternal

That's the
Nature of his
"Freewill" and

That's the
Confidence in
His possibilities

No wonder,
Human indeed is
An "Intellectual
Mysticism;" dares
To reach out to the
Realm of uncertainty,
As always...

Our Vows

Recall
The sacred
Vows and
Do remember
We're in love
Forever

Remember
The days of
Grief and joy
We faced being
A single soul

How
Do you forget?
The reality of
You and I meant
To be forever

Why
This betrayal
When we just
Begun a happy
Journey

Why
Drop off from
The set destiny
We'd dream
All this time?

Will to
Live

I think
Not because,
"I exists," but

I hold
My meditative
Spirit intact

I believe
Not because,
"I accept," but

I explore
The meaning
With a clarity of
The mind

I am focused
To ascend from
Known to the
Unknown even
My time is brief

I know,
This life may be
My last chance and
The journey seem
Many million miles
Still to be rolled…

New Direction

Any
Discourse be
Endeavored with
An open-mind;
Leading toward
Truth

Any
Belief either
Religious or
Otherwise be driven
By the spirit of tolerance
And understandings of
Others

The blueprint
Of humanity be in
Harmony with the
Whole and where
Peace and Cooperation
Be the prime movers…

Moral Call

Is it not
Time to get ready
And walk off the
Corrupted state of
The mind

Is it
Not time to
Rid off the guilt
And grief of our
Collective sins

Come,
Let's celebrate
New awareness

Yes, come
And join the new
Vision for a change

Let's just
Rewrite a new
Experience of our
Kind

Let's simply
Flush out the old
Thoughts and be reborn
With a new attitude of
"Oneness…"

Humanity Above All

Man
Must live in
The state of
Inspiration
Always

Life
Is to be won
By fearlessness
And clarity of the
Mind

Time
To be calm and
Alert and
Knowing where's
The right direction

If religion
Is driven by sheer
Revenge and violence,
It must be discarded,
At once

Let's shape up
For a bright future
Of our children and
Theirs to come…

Dignity

Have we
Ever thought,
“We’re
The time travelers
Passing through
Eternity

Have we
Ever realized,
“We’re deathless
Moral beings;
Gifted
To this petite
Planet Blue”

Have we
Ever awakened
To the fact,
“We’re the
Extension of
The First Cause!”

Immortal

Sweet Heart,
Just to
Let you know,
"We're the
Total reality

Yes,
Dear Heart,
"We're
Evolving through
Eternity and
We shall be
Forever"

Yes,
Sweet smile
That's the way I
See our love going
Beyond ordinary
Human feelings"

So
I ask you to
Be mine forever
Even death says,
"Hello"

We Dare

When all is
So perfect and
Simple
To understand

Why keep
Drowning into the
Complexities of
Our brief time

Let's
Unleash the grand
Intuitive force and
Experience it all,
Instantly

Without
Any thesis,
Hypothesis or
Theory of any sort

Let's
Begin a new journey
To know the genuine
Truth and be the
Enlightened Universe
Ourselves…

Contextual

If there is
Responsibility,
In that case,
“Freedom” got
An ethical value

If there is
Understanding,
In that case,
“Harmony” got
A better chance

If there is
God,
In that case,
“Humanity
Would be one
Moral Reality”

Well, that’s
How Truth
Rules and

That’s
How human
Dignifies his/her
Awakened Soul…

Be Who You're

Don't read
What's been
Written, but know
The essence

Don't listen
To their pep talks,
Just measure their
Experience

Don't believe,
All that's told
By pious ones,

Simply be
Aware of their
Distortion

Don't let
Others govern
The state of
Your mind

For that is
You're "Freewill"
Let it define your
Truth

While walking
Through
The zigzag trail…

An Instinct

I still
Remember your
First smile when
We accidentally
Collided in that
One helluva formal
Party alright

Thought
You're mad and
Ready to slap, instead
You laughed out the
Crisis on the spot

Even,
You were
Willing
To dance with
Me whole night

I intuitively
Knew, you're the
One

Who will be
Dancing;
Much longer than
That evening at the
Hotel Mirage

So glad that
Dream has turned
Into our joint
Reality since then…

Off the Slumber!

No matter
What,
“Existence must
Be driven by my
Core essence”

That’s been
The first line of
Every new chapter
Of my ride along
This rough terrain

While
Am on the
Highway of
My quest let me
Be unstoppable

I now
Know, “Each is
A power of
The mind” ready
To take a giant leap
When he is
Awakened on time…

Off the
Mark!

It may well
Be quite crazy
To think,

"We're
Cropped-up from
One big illusion,
Called, *Nothingness"*

We keep on
Being born over and
Again in many different
Shapes and forms, yet
We never change our
Basic nature for
Some odd reason

We believe
To understand
Mysteries of the Self
And the surrounding world,
Still we fail to grasp with
Our common-sense

Perhaps,
We're just recycling
Intelligent worms trapped
Into the ever spinning
Nothingness!

Welcome

When
The last breath
Bids, “Goodbye”
They say it’s
Over

I say,
“No. It’s the
Left over Urn
From where
A rose bud
Pops-up on the
Scene

Life, Nature
And the Soul all
Are eternal
Holistic reality

So, nothing
Is gone;
“No need to bid
Anyone so-long,
Just “Welcome,
Them always”

Gaia

Once
Earth was
So green and many
Species lived well

Once
Water was
So clean and there
Was fresh air to
Breath

Wild horses
Freely roamed
The rolling hills

And there
Was no modern
Human anywhere

Yes,
That was
When
Mother Nature
Smiled and was
In harmony with
All That Is.

Reality
As Is

History,
What a magic,
Albeit a
"Mirror Image"
Of our choices
And deeds

History
Reminding
Always, our
Collective
Weaknesses
And strengths

History,
Never a friend
Of Conscience;
Hiding many
Sins

History
Reminding,
"Why its
Necessary to
Change the
Deadly course…"

Life
In Motion

Against
All odds,
We
Got to be
The story of
Inspiration

As
We climb the
Mountain with
Moral intention

Let's
Be firm
With the spirit
To keep on
Illuminating

Let each
Step takes us
Away from chaos
And disorder

Let each
Be an
Awakened
Gift of clarity
While we
Climb the
Steep Mountain…

Cross Road

In this
Holistic reality
Where all is one
And one only

Where as
In the
Struggle of
Existence; no
Ones exception

In this
Time of
Uncertainty
And corrupted
State of the mind

Collective
Survival is the
Prime challenge

In this
Milieu of
Anxiety and
Fear; is it
Not time to
Open-up
Our hearts and
Change the track!

Young Braves

Young braves,
Be sure to hold on
Your identity and
Know the solemn
Goal well

Young minds,
Do you realized
Your possibilities
And moral strengths

I say,
Resolve you're self
And be free from the
Dogmatic restraints

Let you
Be creative in
Your endeavors
To succeed

Let you
Be the catalyst
To lift humanity
To the higher order
Of tolerance and
Understanding;
Meeting your
Waiting Truth...

Our Story

As I stand
Alone before
This vastness of
The illumined
Universe

And, when
I spot the two
Shining stars up
There once so close;
Now separating with
Great regret

Surprised
By their mirroring
The story of you and me;
Shining just like them
Once and suddenly,
Separating from one
Another for good

While
Standing alone
Before this mighty
Blue Sea

I am hit by
The memory-waves,
But am determined
To roll forward with a
Renewed dream and
Be the winner, again…

Take
Note

When
We're
Children, time
Went well in
Exploring, playing
And learning

In youth
We turned
Blue and bit
Impatience
And aggressive
Alright

In mid-years,
We're
Over ambitious,
Arrogant and victims
Of greed

In winter
Years,
We begin
To remember, "Our
Follies," but then its
Too late go for a
Second take…

Conundrum

Let's
Just seize the
Moment while
We're here for
A brief

We're
Simply bouncing
Specks going up
And down through
The timelessness
That we don't know
So well

Let's
Just take a moment
To grasp the nature
Of this holistic all
That is

Indeed,
We're essentially
The lost spirits;
Revolving ceaselessly
Between life, death and
Rebirth and still we don't
Understand, "Why?"

Freewill

Wonder,
If path to
Serenity is my
Essence in action

An action
That's powered
By moral courage
To turn dream into
Reality, at once

Then
Why am I
Lost in these
Vicissitudes of
Existence

Let I
Awake and
Clarify the
Very meaning of
My essence at last!

A Jolt

Why keep
Rotting into this
Fragmented mindset
Of God when He's
The Only One

Why
Keep destroying
The future of our
Wonderful kids when
All is so beautiful and
Green

Why
Be victims of
The seven sin when
We're gifts of the
Enlightened mind

Why wait,
Let's unleash
All potentialities
And actualized
Our collective Will
And be far better than
What we've been...

Soul
Singing

We need
Boldness to
Journey together
Toward the
Unknown

We must
Know we're
Evolving reality;
Spinning with
Myriad thoughts
And riddles

No matter
Whatever
The odds

Let's
Learn to be at
The center of our
Moral Being…

Universal Speak

How do we
Bring forth a steady
Societal order with peace
While fighting through
The nasty storms of
Violence's', wars and
Greed

How do we
Clean-up the corrupt
State of our minds and
Pave a right direction
To future generations

These are
The challenges to
Be resolved with
Common-sense and
Certain foresight

Time to
Walk the walk and
Be silent and move the
Needle to the North…

Life
Medley

Lovers
Caught between
Laughs and tears
And not knowing
Where is the escape
From the cage

Modern
Humans too
Trapped between
Old habits and new
Techno thinking
And not knowing
Where is the right
Balance to make it
Through

Future
Belongs to the
Young, but they
Got to discover
Where is well-
Balanced harmony
And rhythm to be free
From blunders of
The past…

High &
Low

We're
The reality,
Always

Yes, we're
The unity of
Wholeness

That is
What the truth
Is all about

That is
What the pursuit
Of life is all about

The idea
Is simple as is,
But reality in action
Remains stubbornly
So unforgiving,
It seems…

North
Star

For
Darkness
Never
Goes away, if
There is no
Sunrise

And
Only true
Measure of a
Genuine being is
The integrity of
His mind

Let
Human spirit
Stand tall in this
Stygian night of the
Twenty-one and

Let him
Cast light every
Where and in every
Whichever way…

Silent Song

Listen
My child,
"Don't be shy
And run away from
Others for all are
Equal in their
Potential and dream"

Listen
My young brave,
"Don't ever undermine
Your inner strength for
You're the owner of
Your destiny"

Listen
My long-time
Pal, "Keep the
Spirit going well
For you've been the
Courage itself"

Listen
Dear child,
"Time to wake up
Be the winner
In the game…"

The Trail

Who
Knows?
Whatever may be
State of intelligent
Life elsewhere

Hamm,
Let see
What we've been
Doing with our
Mixed bag of some
Good and some not

Let's just
Endeavor to
Measure depth of
Our compassion
For a change

Let's free
Ourselves from
Imperfections and
Be the real intelligent
Beings once again…

Prayer

To be
In unity and
Harmony

To be
The manifest
Beauty and
Truth and

Let life
Leap forward
To the right
Destiny

To be
Bold and
Alert

To be
Silent to
Stand firm

To be
Calm and
Be the steady
Mind ever…

Inseparability

Only
Soul is the
Ultimate judge
Of it all

Let
The mind be
Eye and

Let it
Keep clarity of
Conceptuality,
Alright

This
Existence is
All subjective
Inferences and

Never
Reaching
The state of,
"Witnessing
Consciousness"

That is
The challenging
Issue yet to be
Resolved...

The Big Q

At times,
I feel, “Reality
Must be an empty
Sphere without a
Meaning at all”

Even it’s
Filled with infinite
Curiosities and
Creativity,
Why remain
So ignorant

Is it not
My freedom
To think or is it
My negligence

Man
Invented myths
And divinely entity
To decipher the
Truth of it all

Yet,
His journey
Rolls on with
Countless conflicts
Riding with
False narratives…

Eternal

Let's face
The reality
Dear,
We're in
Love forever

Yes sweetie,
There is no
Escape, but
Keep singing
The eternal song

Come,
Dear Life,
We're born to be
Ever

Let's
Rejoice,
Let's
Celebrate our
Time

Let's
Be in the realm
Of love forever,
Forever…forever…

Weird
Way!

What if
We're either an
Ending urn and
Nothing more

Or just
Sticking around
In varying shapes
And forms

I mean,
Between the
Endless game of
Birth and death

What if
We're
Holographic
Projections

I mean,
What if we're
Trapped into this
Accidental reality
Against our will
Or what!

On the Run

Let's
Keep running
Even million
Miles or more

Let's
Keep knocking
The unknown 'til
We get the
Answer on time

Let's
Keep cleaning up
The historic mess
We've been in for
Many millennia
For sure

Yes,
'Let's gather up
Inner strength and
Empower our
Will to win million
Dreams of our time…

All in
Flux

All seems
To be in flux,
All going
In cycles after
Cycles without
A good end

What's
The reason for
Not knowing,
"Where we're
Heading through
The dark clouds"

What's
The reason,
"Why our kind
Hasn't woke up
To the rising
Entropy;
Knocking our
Knuckle heads!"

Unstoppable

Human
Dignity is the
Most precious
Ethical aesthetic

Let every
Being fight for
It unto death

Moral
Duty is the
Foundation of
Our meaning

Let every
Brave soul stand
To defend it to
Their end

Human
Alone defines;
To be the crusader
Of his worthy birth

Let him
Conquer the
Mind and be the
Truth of it all to the
End…

Juggernaut

When
Known and
Known collides,
Curiosity kicks-in
And the quest begins

While
Drowning into
Such a challenging
Sea of debates, doubts
And subjectivity

All seems
So nebulous and
Clarity remains a
Distant call

Yet,
Intelligent
Being
never gives up
For he alone is the
Paradigm shift and

The unknown
Keeps revealing
Inch by inch in
Return…

What do I Know

It’s your
Care and love
They kept me
Alive
With a meaning
Of my life

Yes dear,
It’s your
Sacrifices and
Inspiration gave
Power to our
Journey alright

Glad,
We’re two hearts;
Breathing through
Our love and laugh

Yes,
Dear you’re
The dream turned
Into my reality alright

Yes indeed,
You’ve been shining
Hope and happiness,
For all I know for sure…

Declaration

What If
I dare say,
"All creation seems
A silent prisoner of
My thoughts"

What if,
I dare say,
"All beliefs are
Nothing but the
Conceptuality of
Human invention,
Only!"

Our
Thoughts are the
Source of it all
Our
Creativity is the
Power behind it
All

And,
"Freewill" is the
Only force to
Leap higher than
Where we've been
Thus far…

“I” Matters

I am
A moving
Storm barreling
Through the
Flux of growth
And change

I am the
Willing spirit;
Unfolding the
Power of my
Very essence

Yes,
I am the whim
Who’s caught by
The Unknown of
All That Is

Damn right,
I am ready to
Reckon my truth
Before am no more
On the blessed scene…

Swimmers

Keep
Widening the
Circles of your
Consciousness ‘til
You’ve touched the
Core reality, at last

Keep
Flying through
Creative thoughts
And grasp, “Being
Becoming” for sure

Keep
Dancing till
You’ve arrived to
The Temple of your
“Moral Being,” at last…

Flashes

Flashing
Thoughts keeps
Bouncing back and
Forth every now and
Then

As am
One of the
Riders sharing
The world with
Few of my whims

Anyway,
Let me dare
Express it all:

"History though
A great story,
Why still no real
Beauty in the
Heart of man,
Today?"

I mean,
"How long the
Façade shall rule
The mind that is
So creative and
Quite
Intelligent too!

Old Habit Never Dies

"How long
Is the journey
To the dream world,
Pa?"

"Son, it's
Very long, but
You can cut it short"

"How, Pa?"

"Before we begin,
Let you prepare a
Right attitude and
A clear plan"

"You mean, be
Positive and know
Well each turning
Point"

"That's right, but
Where did you learn
That smart answer?"

"Pa you won't
Believe it, but it's
From Ma!"

Well, Pa remained
Speechless and kept
The cart rolling without
Any further response…

Aporia

They say,
We say and
All together says,
"He's One. He's
Many or He's just
None"

That's been
Glowing Aporia
Since emergence
Of intelligent beings

They say,
We say and
All together says,
"Life got a meaning.
For others, it
Doesn't..."

That's the
Pursuit of big
Thinkers for a long
Meanwhile clarity
Is still waiting
In the wing...

Green *vs* Greed

First
The seed is
Planted and
Slowly growing
With time

Roots
Stabilize the
Little tree and
Getting taller
Through the flow
Of seasons

Now,
Branches pop up
Bringing leaves,
Flowers and juicy
Fruits

The big tree
Giving shelter to
Many birds, insects
And primates

Yes, the green
Tree giving many
Goodies to humans

And, in turn
He keeps destroying
The whole forests for
His petite greed…

Spinning Wheel

Our
Coming
To this
Insignificant
Speck
In the
Universe,

Paradoxically,
Seems to have a
Big significance:

Is it the
The divinely
Invented notion
That is been
A conundrum or
An answer to
All that we're
Seeking?

And
That seems
One of the
Grand mysteries
Yet to free us
From the struggle
We've been in…

Wounded Souls

Those
Beautiful
Memories still
I hold 'em today

Yes, when
We were young
And bit crazy
Alright

Yes, those
Were
The shining
Days when
We were never
Afraid
To fall in love

Then war
Broke out and
We're separated
Against our will and
Time robbed us
In the end

Now,
You're no more,
Your loving smile and
Beauty is left behind
Singing the same old
Song in my heart…

Explorer

Go where
Harmony of the
Mind is with all
Others

That is,
Go fight evil
Where ever
It is

Yes, go for
The dream of
Your life today

No point
Being in
Despair and
Keep
Complaining

Time to
Arise and go
After your own
Truth today…

Determined Will

Dear lady,
Let's dance
With the flow
Of our dreams

Yes,
Let's roll
With the glow
Of our new
Confidence

Don't worry
Of the
Dark clouds,
Just stay
Close to my
Heart and keep
The journey
Going

I say again,
"Keep on
Dancing close to
My heart with
All your endless
Flow of love only…"

Song
Forever

OM is the
First vibrations
When the universe
Awoke from its
Slumber after a long

OM is the
Cosmic sound
Heard by the
Enlightened minds
Even today

OM is the
Rhythms soothing
The soul so silently
Ever

OM is the
Left over resonances
Of the holistic universe

OM perhaps
An acoustic version
Of the vibrating strings

Om what an
Eternal Sound of
Reason even science
Is realizing it's
Beauty and truth, today…

The Premise

Brahman,
Honestly is
A perpetual
Consciousness

No it's
Not a divided
Entity at all, but
The ultimate
Unity forever

Brahman
Means
All-inclusiveness,
All-inspiration and
All-awakening
Throughout multi-
Universe

Brahman,
From where
The meaning of
Truth serves the
Human conceptuality

Brahman,
What a metaphysical
Abyss to facilitate
Clarity to the struggling
Intelligent beings…

Purity

We're
Temporal beings
Spinning into the
Holistic sphere of
What is and what is
Not

We're
The periodic
Flares emanating
From ever burning
Universe

We shall
Live and die and
Live again for the
Set destiny yet to be
Understood

We're
The moral gifts
Born over and again
To experience;

The purity
Of our total
Humanity,
"Who we're and
What
We ought to be."

"I," An Idea

Only in the
State called, "I"
Is the owner of
My truth alive

Only in the
State of
"Nothingness,"
All emerges for
A brief and soon
Disappears

Only in this
Dynamic state of
Growth and change,
"I" keeps climbing
To the realm of
My solemn bliss

That is,
"Nothingness"
Where "I" is the
Authentic meaning,
At rest…

Not Yet

Glorious
Glimpses casting
Shadows from the
Past to the present;

Challenging
To think of the
Future in a hurry

No point
Ignoring the state
Of fate we're in
No point
Being arrogant
In the situation
We're in

No point
Cheering ourselves
When despair and
Uncertainty are the
Dominant theme

No way,
We can quit the
Historic
Humiliation of our
Very being

Let's find
The causes of
Our suffering and take
Necessary responsibility
While we're still
On the scene…

Enigmatic

If we are
Accidental then
It's okay to be
No different than all
Other animals

But then,
The question arises,
"Why we can reason,
Plan and envision
Future, now and then"

If we are
Intentional creatures,
Then it's not okay to be
Driven by the seven sin

And yet,
We just follow the
Same old track: envy,
Vanity, selfishness,
Greed and so on

I mean, why
We refuse to change
The stubborn
"Human nature with
Our moral freewill!"

JAGDISH J. BHATT, PhD

Brings 45 years of academic experience including a post-doctorate research scientist at Stanford University, CA. His career publications of scientific, educational and literary are nearly 100 including authorship of over 50 books.

www.ingramcontent.com/pod-product-compliance
Lightning Source LLC
LaVergne TN
LVHW050550160826
845677LV00011B/2256

* 9 7 9 8 3 6 6 9 2 6 7 6 8 *